Why Covid

scares the world

The story of an invisible tiny virus

told by fotolulu

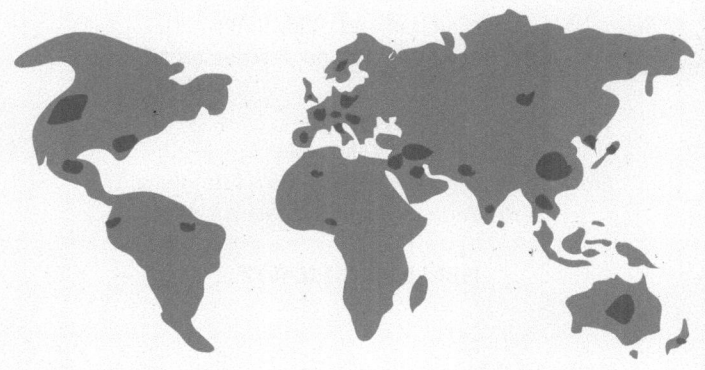

Imprint

Bibliographic information from the German National Library:
The German National Library lists this publication
in the German National Bibliography;
detailed bibliographic data can be found on the Internet at
www.dnb.de.

Production and publishing:
BoD - Books on Demand, Norderstedt

1st edition
© 2020 fotolulu
Illustrations & text: fotolulu · www.fotolulu.com
Translation to English: William Ying

ISBN: 9783751904872

Content

Why Covid scares the world

The story of an invisible tiny virus

Many years ago, a small virus called Covid was sitting in a cave in the Chinese province of Hubei. The cave was dark, it was uncomfortably cold, and Covid was alone. A large colony of bats lived on the cave ceiling. They were horseshoe bats, a very sociable bat species. Every night the bats flew out of the cave to hunt insects. Covid was alone in the cave and longed for some warmth.

One morning Covid snuck up to the cave ceiling and waited for the bats to come home. When the sun rose, the horseshoe noses came back. Mr. Wang and Ms. Li landed right next to Covid. They hung their back legs on the cave ceiling, licked their fur and talked about their hunting successes.

It was nice and warm between the bats and Covid made a decision. He crawled down Wang's legs unnoticed, slid over the smooth flying skin, and landed in Mr. Wang's mouth.

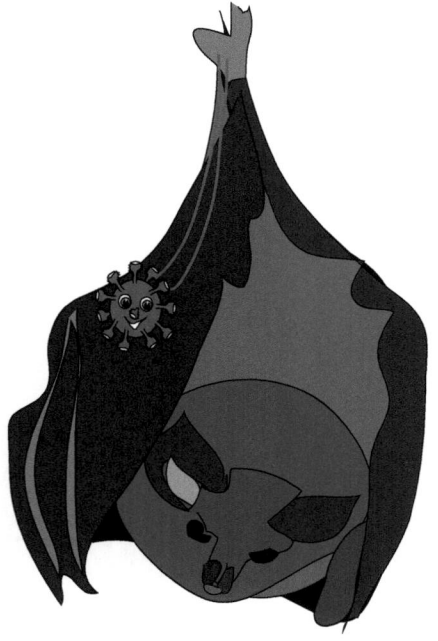

Mr. Wang didn't notice anything because Covid is so tiny that you can only see him under a very powerful microscope. Covid made himself comfortable in Mr. Wang's warm mucous membranes and was happy. He lived in Mr. Wang's warm body for weeks. He went on an insect hunt every night and hung head down from the cave ceiling during the day. Everything was actually fine, because Covid was no longer cold and was in company.

Friends need to come

What Covid lacked, however, were real friends with whom he could play with. Covid explored Mr. Wang a little from the inside and discovered a host cell in his lungs. The special thing about this cell was that Covid could dock onto it like a rocket connecting to the international space station.

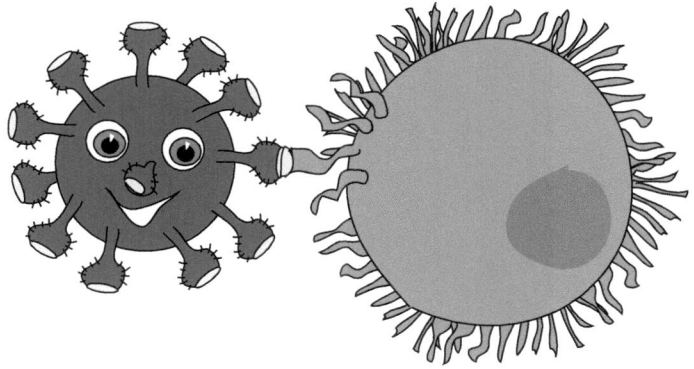

Now Covid was able to enter the host cell and Covid could replicate itself in the nucleus of the cell. Covid was surprised, he hadn't expected that.

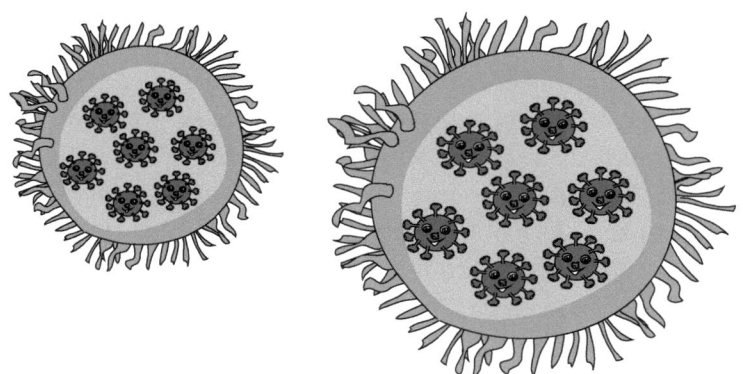

After a short time there were hundreds of little Covids and they all looked the same. Covid was thrilled and he had a huge party in Mr. Wang's lungs.

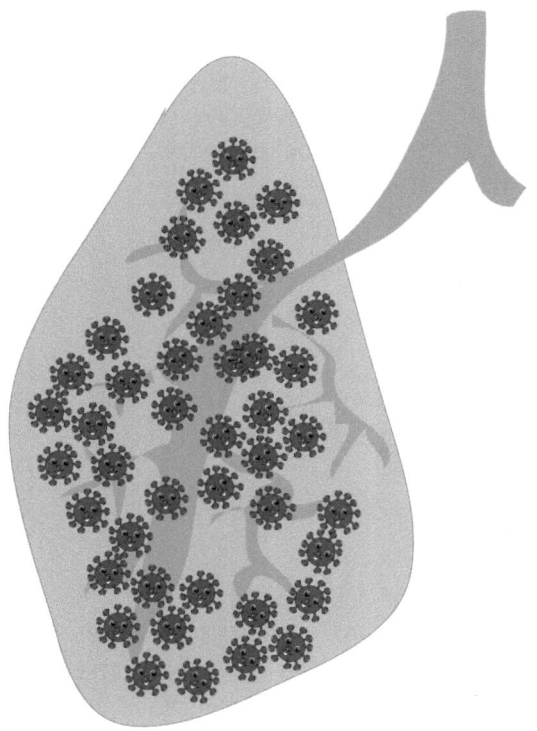

When the party was really going on, Mr. Wang suddenly had to cough. There was such a strong gust of wind that many of the party guests were torn away. They were catapulted through the windpipe, into Mr. Wang's throat, and because his mouth was open, they flew into the cave. Some were able to cling to the many bats hanging around. Those who hadn't made it landed on the cave floor and froze to death after a short time.

Covid was lucky; he had clung to a vesicle in time. In the days that followed, Covid's life was accompanied by many of Wang's coughing fits. Covid knew the signs of a coughing fit and could always get to safety in time. Mr. Wang's coughing fits gradually infected all the bats in the cave. Now there was a constant cough in the cave and all the bats were a little annoyed.

At some point, Mr. Wang and the other bats' coughing fits disappeared, and Covid and all of his relatives were able to live in peace inside the bats.

One day, Covid heard Mr. Wang say to Ms. Li, "Did you hear? The goshawk from the edge of the forest died yesterday." Ms. Li asked, outraged, "Isn't that the one who ate our neighbor Mr. Wung?" Mr. Wang nodded:

"Right, that's the bat-eater." "But what did he die of?" Ms. Li wanted to know.

"It is said that he died of pneumonia caused by some virus." Covid considered for a moment and realized that his relatives could have been responsible for the death of the crested goshawk. "It's mean when a stranger eats your home," thought Covid.

In the following years, such incidents occurred again and again. Birds of prey and snakes that had eaten some of the bats had to pay for it with their lives.

Covid wondered why the bats' predators died, but the bats themselves have been cheerfully living. He watched Mr. Wang's behavior a little more closely and noticed that he had a special metabolism. Mr. Wang had a very busy life. At up to 160 km / h, he flies around for hours every night looking for insects. His little heart beats a thousand times a minute. In order for Mr. Wang to do this every night, he has to save energy elsewhere.

So Mr. Wang also has a very slow immune system, which is supposed to fight viruses. But that costs a lot of energy and so Mr. Wang developed another strategy. The immune cells are very slow and also allow Covid to enter the host cell. There, however, he does not destroy the intruder, which would also cost too much energy, but keeps the intruder at bay. So Covid and Mr. Wang can live together wonderfully.

The intruders

One morning people with huge landing nets came into the cave. Covid, Mr. Wang, and Ms. Li did not feel good about this. As it turned out, they were right to feel this way. The men caught hundreds of horseshoe noses from the cave ceiling and put them in sacks. It was not a pretty sight and panic spread. Mr. Wang and Ms. Li were caught, and so was Covid. The men drove with the full bags to the wild animal market in Wuhan. Once there, they killed the bats and offered them for sale. When one of the men killed Mr. Wang, Covid became angry and made a revenge plan.

As Mr. Wang breathed his last breath, Covid did not hold on to one of the alveoli, but stood in the gust of wind. The last breath was enough to throw Covid out of Mr. Wang's mouth and he landed in the man's mouth.

Covid immediately made his way inside, all the way to the lungs, and docked there at a host cell. Covid multiplied furiously and after a short time millions of virus relatives attacked the bat killer's lungs.

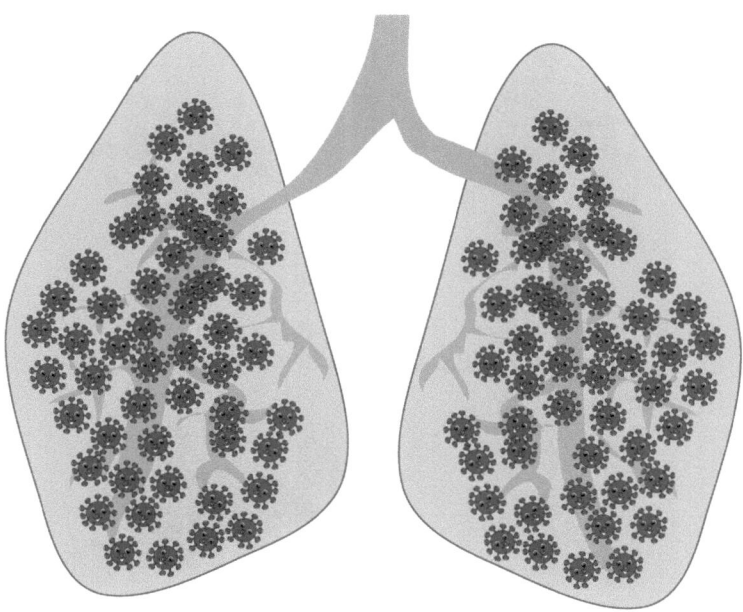

The revenge campaign

The man fell ill and developed severe pneumonia. This happened to everyone he had coughed near in the past two weeks or with whom he had close contact. Covid was furious. His revenge plan worked and the man who killed Mr. Wang also died. Covid also died with this man. His relatives mourned him and now decided to avenge Covid's death.

After Covid was buried, madness began. Billions of Covid's relatives went to war. Covid himself would never have wanted this. He just wanted to protect himself and his host, Mr. Wang.

So the vengeance of the virus got out of control and every virus wore a black band with the imprint of Covid in memory of Covid.

The year of the rat

The revenge campaign came at a very unfortunate time. In China, everyone was busy preparing the most important folk festival. The Chinese New Year, also called the Spring Festival, was imminent. The Chinese follow the lunar calendar and therefore New Year is not on January 1 in China, but in this case on January 25, 2020.

The legend of the Chinese New Year

In ancient times there was a malicious monster with sharp teeth and horns called Nian. Hiding in the dark sea all year round, Nian would go ashore at the end of the lunar year and hunt people and their cattle. For this reason, people fled to the remote mountains each year before the New Year to avoid Nian's attack.

However, one day when an old man visited the village, everything was about to change. Nian didn't come this year. The old man said to the villagers, "The monster is easy to scare. It especially does not like the color red. It fears loud noises and unknown creatures. Tonight you are wrapping the village in red with red jewelry on every door. Makes noise with drums, loud music and fireworks. And protect your children. Give them masks and lanterns ".
The residents did just that and Nian was never seen again.

In Chinese, New Year translates to "Guo Nian", which means "conquer the Nian". That's exactly what the residents did.

Part of the New Year's tradition is decorating the houses with red decorations. The streets are filled with the sound of music, drums and fireworks.

The year of the rat began on January 25, 2020. This has to do with the Chinese signs of the zodiac. There are twelve animals and each year is represented by one of these animals. The signs of the zodiac consist of rat, ox, tiger, rabbit, dragon, snake, horse, goat, monkey, rooster, dog and pig. In this order, they are repeated every twelve years.

Each animal is assigned certain properties:

The rat is very curious imaginative, versatile, witty and can adapt to any situation.

The buffalo is known for his hard work reliability, strength and determination.

The tiger is brave, cheeky, unpredictable and very headstrong. The tiger can face any challenge.

The rabbit is gentle, calm, alert, friendly, patient and responsible.

The dragon, the only mythical creature, is the strongest animal. It symbolizes dominance and ambition.

The snake is considered silent, intelligent and wise.

The horse is especially lively, active and energetic.

The goat has a gentle Temperament, is a little shy, but compassionate and balanced.

The monkey is witty, playful, curious, refined and likes to goof off.

The rooster is very mindful, brave and confident. He is open, sincere and always appears attractive and pretty.

The dog is considered loyal sincere, obliging, kind and prudent.

The pig is hardworking compassionate and generous.

The Chinese New Year is a celebration of families, who of course also visit each other. The Chinese believe that starting the New Year well will lead to a happy and prosperous year and so thousands of people working far from their families made their way home.

More and more people in the city of Wuhan fell ill and some died due to the consequences from the lung disease. People became nervous and reported the incidents to the World Health Organization (WHO). China sealed off the entire area around Wuhan immediately to prevent the spread of the disease. Scientists and doctors went in search of the culprit. A patient's saliva sample ended up in a laboratory and a scientist took a closer look at it under a very powerful microscope.

The scientist was surprised because he found a virus that was very similar to an already known virus. At that time, many people fell ill with a SARS virus and the new vi¬rus now looked similar. The scientist gave it the name SARS-CoV-2. Since this name was difficult to re-member, the virus was eventually called the Coronavi-rus. Ho¬wever, the scientists did not like this and after another scientist discovered the black band with the label Covid, he called the virus Covid-19, because the virus broke out in December 2019.

The little relatives of Covid were happy with the name, because now their hero was known all over the world.

One relative was particularly proud. It was Covid's first "twin", Covid-Two, who had survived in a young Chinese woman. She was visiting Wuhan, but had to go home after a week. She had shown no symptoms and no one knew that Covid-Two lived in her. The woman named Li Liang lived carefree in Beijing, the capital of China. At that time, an epidemic was declared in Wuhan and no one was allowed to enter or leave. Thousands of people became infected in no time and there was no end in sight.

The trip to Europe

Ms. Li Liang and Covid-Two didn't notice much because they lived 1,200 kilometers away in a small apartment in Beijing. Ms. Li Liang worked in a factory that produced automobile parts for the whole world. One day, she was sent to Germany by her boss. There was a seminar in which she needed to take part in.

Ms. Li Liang booked a flight, hotel, and made her way to Germany. Covid-Two traveled with her, but had multiplied a million times in the past week. Ms. Li Liang had a mild cough, so she infected her family, some work colleagues, the taxi driver who brought her to the airport, and some passengers on the plane. Ms. Li Liang spread the virus and it was able to cross several national borders. Some of the passengers who became infected flew to Italy, others to Iran, America and so on.

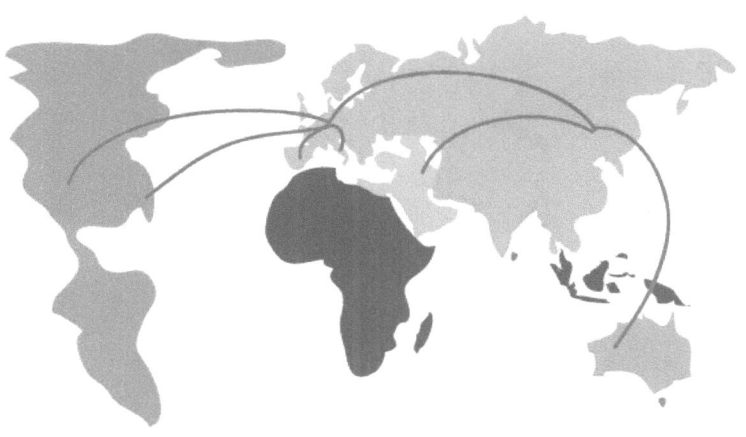

Covid-Two landed with Ms. Li Liang in Frankfurt and they drove to the hotel. The seminar lasted three days and during this time some seminar participants were infected. Covid-Two was transferred by Ms. Li Liang due to a coughing fit. He now lived in Mr. Müller, who lives in a small village in North Rhine-Westphalia. Covid-Two lived and multiplied in Mr. Müller, who knew nothing about it.

The virus also arrived in Germany at a very unfavorable time. It was Carnival and Mr. Müller loves to dress up and celebrate Carnival. So Mr. Müller attended a carnival celebration together with Covid-Two and his relatives. Every carnival event includes asking for "Bützchen", which is when the partygoers call for a kiss. Of course, that was bad because the virus spread very easily and quickly.

Pandemic alert

At the same time, there were more and more reports of people getting sick from many countries around the world and so the World Health Organization (WHO) decided to declare a pandemic.

If a large number of people become infected with a virus, this is called an epidemic. As long as the spread is limited to a small area or country, it remains an epidemic. However, if the disease spreads across countries or even across continents, it is called a pandemic.

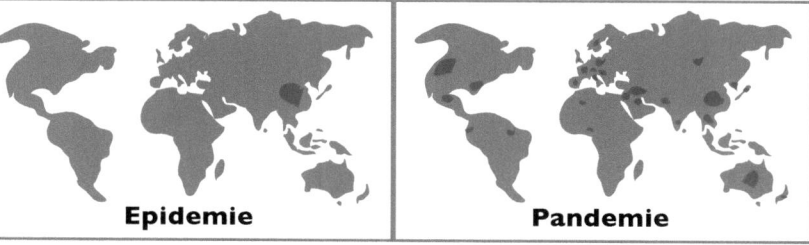

Epidemie   **Pandemie**

Pandemics have been around for hundreds of years. The best-known pandemics in history were the plague, Spanish flu, swine flu, bird flu and HIV. Because we know about these pandemics that have killed millions of people, we have become very careful. That is why there are strict rules set out by the World Health Organization (WHO) in an international pandemic plan. According to that, each country has drawn up its own pandemic plan. In Germany, the National Pandemic Plan sets out the rules for protecting oneself and each other and is updated regularly.

Such a plan is important because nobody knows when, where and in what form a new viral disease breaks out. It's about stopping new infections in the event of an outbreak and finding a vaccine as soon as possible.

Daily life with Covid

Many measures were taken to curb the spread. The most important thing is sticking to some rules. With simple measures everyone can help protect themselves and others from infectious diseases.

The most important hygiene tips:

Sneeze or cough into the crook of your arm or into a tissue - and then dispose of the tissue into a trash can with a lid.

Keep your hands away from your face - avoid touching your mouth, eyes, or nose with your hands.

Keep enough distance from people who have a cough, runny nose or fever - also due to the ongoing flu and cold wave.

Avoid touching (e.g. shaking hands or hugging) when greeting or saying goodbye to other people.

Wash your hands regularly with water and soap for a sufficient amount of time (at least 20 seconds) - especially after you blow your nose, sneeze, or cough.

What else can help stop the spread?

Stay at home as often as possible. Read a good book, learn for school, paint or make great things.

You shouldn't visit grandma and grandpa now, because older people and people with chronic illnesses are particularly at risk. Call them, write an email or have a video chat.

If you meet friends or neighbors, keep your distance. Shaking hands and hugs must be avoided. There are certainly other cool ways to greet each other, which can be done at a safe distance of 1 to 2 meters.

If someone in your family is ill, the whole family must be very careful and should avoid any contact with other people.

If you are well, you can help others. You can help grandma and grandpa, elderly neighbors or friends who are not allowed to leave their apartment. You can go shopping for them, but then you should put the groceries outside and avoid any direct contact.

How does life go on?

If we manage to stop Covid-Two and his relatives from spreading, Covid's revenge campaign will come to an end.

Do we have to demonize the virus now?

Who is to blame for the pandemic? The seemingly harmless virus? The bats? The bat catchers? The people who eat bats?

The answer is probably that no one can be blamed because it was a series of unfortunate events. Bats have been eaten for hundreds of years and nothing ever happened. They were caught just as long. The bats generally carry viruses and the viruses never attacked humans.

The epidemic was therefore the result of several, coinciding factors. The fact that the epidemic became a pandemic is due to globalization. Not only can people and goods travel easily, the viruses can also cross national borders.

We humans are able to learn and so we should learn from this pandemic. We shouldn't stick to old habits, even if they haven't caused problems for generations. The world is constantly evolving. Animals die out, new species develop and the same can be said for the smallest living things such as viruses and bacteria. We have to live with them, even if they can be a danger to humanity.

List of sources:
https://www.chinarundreisen.com/das-chinesische-fruehlingsfest/
https://www.rki.de/SharedDocs/FAQ
https://www.infektionsschutz.de/coronavirus-sars-cov-2.html

More fotolulu children's books

fotolulu in Florida und auf den Bahamas
Ein lustiger Vogel erkundet für euch die Welt mit der Kamera!

fotolulu
68 Seiten
ISBN-13: 9783752849684
Verlag: Books on Demand

fotolulu in Afrika
Ein lustiger Vogel erkundet für Euch die Welt mit der Kamera

fotolulu
76 Seiten
ISBN-13: 9783735775641
Verlag: Books on Demand

fotolulu auf Sri Lanka
Ein lustiger Vogel erkundet für Euch die Welt mit der Kamera!

fotolulu

56 Seiten
ISBN-13: 9783735723925
Verlag: Books on Demand

www.tier-kids.de
www.fotolulus-abenteuer.de
www.fotolulu.com